THE ALCHEMIST

THE ALCHEMIST

POEMS 2019

CONTENTS

MARCIA M. SALTON

THE RESERVOIR

The water sparkles blue and calm.
Tourists and locals pause to see.

They do not know or don't recall
What lies beneath this tranquil scene.

Our Atlantis. Real. No myth.
Swamped. Swallowed. Seen no more.

Houses, churches, schools, and roads
Deliberately drowned. Did no one care?

People cast out. Lives displaced.
Family birthrights vanished. Gone.

Done for need, for progress, growth.
For strangers in a far-flung place
The water sparkles blue and calm
Masking the death that lies below.

MORNING REFLECTIONS

Nary a ripple on the glass-like lake,
water mimics the shoreline scene.
Geese swim lazily by in pairs,
their goslings in a line behind.
A hawk glides slowly through the air
effortlessly seeking its morning meal.
A beaver breaks the water's surface
then swims under a dock nearby.
The sky is clear and crystal blue
only a stray cloud here and there.
The sun glares morning strong and bright
streaming warmth throughout the house.
I stand with tea cup in my hand
Inhaling the beauty and the calm.

GET THEM DONE

I've so many projects
to get them all done
I've set aside days,
a time for each one.
Some days are so busy
I abandon my plan.
I'll double up next week
that is if I can.
Today is for writing
but my brain is bare.
I'm at the computer
but I just sit and stare.
Tomorrow or next day
sight or sound may inspire.
Right now, it's quite late,
I think I'll retire.

VERTICALLY CHALLENGED

Arms too short, shelves too high,
on tall people I must rely.

Clothes too wide and much too long,
I look like Granny in her sarong.

In my auto, pedals too far,
Way too short to sit at a bar.

Bought high heels a while back,
couldn't walk so took them back.

I've been told petite is cute,
someone please give them a boot.

Can't grow taller, I have tried,
But I get bigger from side to side.

To those of you with longer limbs,
please hold off on all the grins.

Just help me reach the things I want,
without laughter, without taunt.

And I promise no grins or jeers
When people laugh at your big ears.

YEARLY REBIRTH

Winter's past, Spring is here.
The sun is bright, the sky is clear.

The garden store has stuff galore.
I'm like a kid in a candy store.

Seeds and soils and tools and more.
My charge card sees its balance soar.

Ailing back and aching limbs,
eagerly I plant, weed, trim.

I sit on the deck and enjoy the view,
vines and flowers, pink, green, blue.

Too soon it's done and all is brown.
Leaves die, snow falls, Summer's gone.

With time and patience, Winter's past
And Spring arrives again, at last.

MY HYDRANGEAS

Al had a thumb as green as could be.
All that he planted grew magnificently.

But caring for plants made him moan
and groan.
Dropped them in, added water, then left
them alone.

For weeding and trimming on me he relied.
With my dark black thumb, flowers just died.

He was the gardener; it was his domain.
My asking for choices were always in vain.

But one year, my begging and pleading
were heard.
He finally planted the kind I preferred.

Two blue hydrangeas, quite small at first,
Which he watered, trimmed
and carefully nursed.

Each summer now, through my window I see
a bittersweet, poignant, much loved memory.

SQUIRRELLY THOUGHTS

Squirrels soar and jump with ease
like acrobats on a circus trapeze.

From tree to tree they hurriedly go
over clothes lines, high and low.

Down trees, up trees, incredibly fast
I love watching them through window glass.

Not always smart, but very shrewd
nothing stops them from finding food.

Then they hide it, forget it just like me.
Good grief! Maybe I am squirrelly.

Some folks hunt and eat these rodents—
Not my idea of dinner components.

Kentucky burgoo and Brunswick stew?
Enjoy if you wish, not me, thank you.

Cute and mischievous in the trees
not so much when they eat my seeds.

Off my feeder you thieving swine.
This is where I draw the line.

Scat! go way! Your mealtime's done.
Watching you's no longer fun.

LIFE'S STORMS

The summer sun is high and bright.
Our spirits soar and life is good.

All at once there's rain and thunder,
lightning, bleak skies, darkness too.

We look for shelter, hide, withdraw
Until again the sun shines through.

The storms of life are much the same,
striking swiftly, not a clue.

Our spirits wither. Life is bleak.
We evade, avoid, shut out the world.

In time, our wounds are healed, repaired.
The pace is different for each one.

The scars remain, repressed, unseen.
Until reopened now and then.

As sun returns, so we do too.
To life revived, revised, renewed.

PATRICIA DURNEY

MEMORIES OF LOVE

There's a warm place
Below your neck on the side
Where a hollow forms.
I find it by moving
my lips down from your ear
and turning your head ever so slightly
with an upward movement of my lips
to taste the salt of your warm familiar smell
so gently done you never wake.

LADY DELAWARE

She combs her hair and lets it fall into long
shimmering pools among the reeds
and quiet trees.
She lets it fall in cascades of blue whirling eddies
fashioned with foam.
She fastens it to slow the rush, yet boulders fall
broken along the bank.
She ties it into a braid so narrow it slips tamely
through the sand dunes and reeds
of nesting places.
But when she tosses her head and sings
her wild song, her crashing, howling siren song,
the trees mimic and thrash boughs
and leaves against the sky.
Then, she bends her head and her hair falls down
rushing headstrong over the falls—
a drumming torrent through a forest
that holds its breath.
Finally, she rests and turns and twists in a bed
made mute with rocky shelves frozen in ancient
rhythms of upheaval and rebirth.

THE SOUND OF YOU

I love the way you sound the soothing notes
the words that dance, the sighs so deep,
the laugh that giggles.
I love the sound of you.
I love your words,
the rhymical breath
as you rest your head against my chest.
I feel the warmth they speak.
I dream of long summer days.
Always I remember your sound
as others remember beauty,
the scent of rambling rose
like an opiate that fills my soul
I long for the sound of you.

WHAT BUGS ME

The lilacs I pick are never right,
the flowers too loose or too brown.
The branches harbor dark brown bugs
that crawl round and round.

And so, it is with me.
The things I love are never right.
Attachments come too loose, passions grow
too old, and little annoyances
crawl round my mind

GENDER ADVICE

If a woman wants to win
she needs to be very thin.
The less there is of her, the better she will be.

If a woman wants to speak
her words should be meek.
The less there is of her, the better she will be.

If a woman wants to succeed
a manly voice she should heed
The less there is of her, the better she will be.

If a woman is too smart
she had better hide her art.
The less there is of her, the better she will be.

If you're a little woman
then little you will be.
The less there is of you, the smaller you will be.

P.R. GATES

THE OLD DOG

The old dog looked at me, as if to say, "You know
it's raining out?"
I looked at her and replied, "I know."

She gave me that dog look.
Big brown eyes, sad expression.
I said, "I know it's raining. If you could use
the toilet, I'd let you."

The dog sighed. Half human, I swear. She sighed
when she was disgusted, she burped after
she ate, and of course, she had dog gas
when she ate certain foods. She would not
apologize after the burp and she vacated
the room after the gas
as if she were not the culprit.

"All right", I said. "I'm getting there."
I got off the couch and she lifted her head.
I told my arthritis to behave. She heard me.
She didn't lift the rest of her body until
she saw me put on my rain boots
and get my umbrella.

Finally, she got up off the floor and wagged
her tail. Once. Together, we went into the rain.
She did what she does, in ladylike dog fashion.

We walked back into the house,
where I mentioned to the dog that she reminded
me of the old commercial, "What do you smell?
I smell a wet dog."

Of course, after I toweled her off, she gave me
that dog look again and immediately jumped
on the couch to sit beside me. I sighed
and covered us up with the quilt.
Just the old dog and me.

BURY ME BAREFOOT

Bury me barefoot,
It's my last request.
I'll dress down and dress
Up to my very best.

Shoes are not wanted
When I go on my quest,
For where I am going,
I won't be a guest.

The sand in my shoes
Is much better afoot.
There will be no housework,
I won't have to cook.

Every mud puddle will have
An invite attached
On my face will be
A smile unmatched

Put me six feet under,
Don't burn me with fire.
Please bury me barefoot,
It's my last desire.

DAMPNESS

Cool and damp
Sun up to sundown.
Not a sliver of sunshine
on this cloudy day.

T-shirt or sweater,
slacks or shorts.
Nothing looks comfortable.
How about a nightshirt?

Doors swollen with moisture.
One won't open
the other won't shut.
Can't break in or break out.

What is worse?
Rain or last year's drought?
My arthritis says dampness
is not the winner in July.

NAPKIN POEM

written on a napkin while waiting for our order

How delicate the birch tree
outside the window.
I see papery bark with dancing branches.
It stands alone on the hill.
Birds and deer visit the ground
it stands upon.
The birch doesn't live forever
like its sister the oak.
A strong wind will take it down.
To watch it sway gently in the wind
is a joy in its own right.

YOU WERE HERE

You were in my thoughts again today,
Suddenly on my mind. I wondered why.
I could hear your laughter
and see the glint in your eye as you teased me.
Your gentle manner made me laugh at myself.
Only you could make me do that, make me find
the humor of me being me.

How can we be so far apart?
I feel as though you are in the same room.
My subconscious mind pushing reality aside.
Perhaps you were with me because I now realize
That everyone is mortal, even you.
I never thought you'd die,
but to me, you never will.

WAITING

They stand in the backyard
Looking at me through the window.
Waiting for their corn.

Their eyes upon me —
Four sets of eyes, sixteen legs.
Beautiful doe eyes, staring.
She stands in the hallway

Waiting to go out in the snow.
Her eyes upon me as she waits.
Two eyes and four legs,
Beautiful dog eyes.

I stand in the parlor,
tired eyes watch the sky.
One set of eyes with two legs
look out the window
stare at falling snowflakes,
waiting for spring to arrive.

All of us waiting for time to pass,
for spring to arrive,
for flowers to pop up,
for fresh grass to eat,
for paths to travel.
Spring takes its time.

FIREFLIES

Tiny specks of light
catch my eye at night
they move from place to place
in the dark, into space.
Lightning bugs or fireflies.
They always catch my eyes.

HE LEFT TODAY

He left today for the big wide world.
Destination miles from home
to start a new job
that he's worked and trained for.

He left today, his mind set.
He and the car both prepared
for a ride into his future
and out of his past.

He left today and left this place.
Why the worrying? He will be fine!
Bringing them up so very easy,
letting them go so very hard.

He left today, this adult child
went out the door.
In my mind I still see and feel
the child he once was.

VERA ATKINS

PASTA IS MY FAVORITE FOOD

Pasta is my favorite food;
I eat it all the time.
It even comes in colors now,
Like yellow, orange and lime.

Spaghetti is the best of all.
I pile my plate up high,
Pour on the sauce and meatballs—
Enough to make me sigh.

Next, I stir it gently,
Shake on some grated cheese.
A little salt and pepper
Will always make me sneeze!

Then I take my fork and spoon
And twirl those strands around,
Put on my apron and my bib
So no mess will be found.

MY TREE

I found a seed and planted it.
Up came a little sprout.
I talked to her and watered her.
She grew up tall and stout.

Now squirrels store their winter food
up in her branches high.
Birds build their nests among her boughs,
then teach their young to fly.

I sometimes sit beneath my tree
when my day's work is done.
She reaches out her loving arms
to shield me from the sun.

When the days grow shorter
and frost is in the air,
her dress will change from green to gold:
A beauty queen so fair.

Thank God for little seedlings
from which great oak trees grow.
Without a hand from Heaven above
We could not make it so.

A SPRING MORNING

The sun came up from behind the hill
like a ball in the clear blue sky.
It shone with warmth of early Spring,
as Winter had just passed by.

Pussy willows like kittens did sit
in the boughs of the willow tree,
and robins warbled their song of joy;
they knew once more they were free.

Daffodils lifted their heads from the ground
to try on their dresses of gold,
and hundreds of butterflies danced in the
breeze, their colorful wings to unfold.

God shows His love in the beauty He paints:
The sunshine, the birds and the flowers—
New life to the Earth after winter's long sleep,
awakened by heavenly showers.

AUTUMN

Days are getting shorter,
frost is in the air,
leaves of brilliant color
are falling everywhere.

Trees now standing naked
as cool breezes blow,
wait for their new coat
of soft and fluffy snow.

Autumn days are sunny,
skies are deepest blue,
moonlight on the water
gives us a lovely view.

Wild geese in formation
flying through the sky,
are heading for a warm place
to pass the Winter by.

We prepare for Winter.
The harvest of the year:
Fruit and nuts and pumpkins
bring us Autumn cheer.

MY SPECIAL PLACE

I have a very special place
beside a babbling brook,
where God's love surrounds me
everywhere I look.

Mountains in the distance
seem to reach the sky,
while clouds like fluffy cotton balls
constantly drift by.

Nearby, a sparkling waterfall
glitters in the light;
when the sun shines through the mist,
behold! a rainbow bright.

Song birds in the treetops
warble all day long,
and bring a happy message
to all who hear their song.

Early in the morning
and at the close of day,
wild deer come to drink the water
and to romp and play.

You can find your special place
if you just look around.
There is no place on this great Earth
where God's love can't be found.

CORA SCHWARTZ

FEBRUARY WIND

(to women who have known true love)

Friday night you are alive again
I strain to hear your whistle
see you burst back into life
in a glorious shower of stars.

Enticed by the wine glass
watching my single, hopeless tear
you speak your wordless wisdom
your heavy hands resting on yellow formica.

Treacherous wind
whips around the northeast corner
creeps through our thin wills
rattles windows like bones.

I'll make tea.
You watch the candle
I lit it for you, my dear.
No Sabbath for us.

Hear the chimes
garbage pails crashing
see your man hanging,
dancing in the Gypsy wind.

We are the last of the last
so take your time.
Warm yourself
on the copper pot.

I ask, "Shall I turn up the heat?"
You answer, "Suffering is good."
I say, "One candle can light the darkness."
You laugh and say, "It always goes out."

A GRANDMOTHER'S BABYSITTING PRAYER

(for the babies taken from their mothers at the border; a snowy afternoon in February, 2019)

Oh,
That all G-d's babies would have:
This pure water
These fresh vegetables
This clean diaper
This sweet milk
These warm pajamas
This shelter from the storm.

BUCHAREST AT NIGHT

Oct. 26, 2008, Hotel Banat
(to my late husband;
a Holocaust survivor who showed me the world)

Your spirit is here in this old hotel room.
Its laughter drifts out through heavy drapes
blends with echoing street sounds below,
sips local wine in the elegant glass
of yesterday, lifts its arms, whistles
to the high carved ceiling.

Dance Rudy.
Dance your own dance.
The one where you pretend
you are what you are not.
The one where you are
what you pretend.

I CAN PRETEND

*(to women on International Women's Day
March 2013 sent from Block Island, R.I.)*

I can pretend
the distant upright boulder
stark on the breakwater's tip
is a woman.

Waves pound her
ocean water floods her eyes
mingles with her tears.

She will never succumb.
As with the tides
she takes it, takes it
again, again.

She faces east
where the sun rises before her
in adoration.

A white seagull rests momentarily
On her crown
Shares the spreading warmth
Watches how her drying tears
Make salt scars on her cheek.

She will wait
for that something on the horizon.
It will arrive
dancing on the high seas
to make her real.

A DYING SURVIVOR

(to my late husband, Rudy)

Laughing
you retreat to starvation
with your sixty-year-old beans.

Laughing
you retreat to scratching
your sixty-year-old lice.

Laughing
you retreat to agonizing Transnystria snow
with your rag-wrapped blue feet.

Laughing
you retreat to the stench of blood, shit,
begging to Adonai.

This time
I cannot bring you back.

MARILYN VASKO LAUFER

RAPTOR

Sharp talons, yellow eyes
Impressive by his size,
Amazing when he flies.
Atop tall maple tree
oblivious to me.
Black, white, wind-blown and free
this hawk-like bird of prey
goes hunting every day,
his hunger to allay:
Osprey.

POETRY

My Gram wrote "old school" poetry:
It had rhythm and rhyme.
Mom did the same thing, in her turn;
I followed suit in mine.

They told a story, shared a thought,
spoke of a tree or bird.
Others related to their words,
could feel what they had heard,

Sharing emotions in few words,
their verse a simple tale
of daily life and conflict, or
a fantasy unveiled.

I love the poems of Robert Frost,
admire Verlaine and Poe.
In classic poetry that lasts,
rhyme was the way to go.

These days some poets choose to use
a form resembling prose,
And when it's time to interpret,
some folks don't really know

Just what those poems are about,
shrouded in mystery,
sophistication seems the goal.
But they do not touch me!

I wonder if some writers are
too Modern? Pseudo? Worse?
Are they not disciplined enough
to create rhyming verse?

Most folks accept that poetry
is used, and rhymed, in song.
Modern, country, rap, or jazz,
No one would say that's wrong !

I once was intimidated
by colleagues who would try
to be enigmatic and deep,
and write in such a way
to challenge readers to debate,
"What does that poem say?"

But now I won't apologize
for my old-fashioned style.
I'll evoke peace, sadness, anger,
make people frown or smile.

There is a place for many modes,
and subjects as diverse
as backgrounds of the writers, who
use rhyme OR write free verse.

The bottom line is this, my friends:
your poem's expressing YOU.

CANOPY

I pass as through a corridor of trees,
On both sides of the road:
Tall, supple,
Leaning together above my head.
Yellow, gold, and tan they stand,
Silent, in solidarity, they are sentry and shield.

Occasionally, a hearty gust of wind, a rustle of
movement,
And a rain of color descends
By ones, and twos, and several at a time.

Too soon, this "rain" will be replaced by winter
snow,
Allowed to pass through the canopy by the naked,
open branches.
Until then, I look forward to my walks
Beneath those wondrous sheltering trees,
As they slowly shed their colorful wardrobe.

It is my delight to slosh through, and trample,
The browning mass of crisp and crinkling leaves,
Amble on as the road curves,
And find out where it leads.

SEND ME YELLOW ROSES

I do not want cut blooms now.
When they die, the musty odor of wilted
vegetation offends.

But when I die, send yellow roses,
If you've a mind to remember me with flowers.

Roses are so sturdily delicate,
vulnerable and honest,
protecting themselves with sharp barbs
while unfolding layer upon fragrant layer
of bashful "getting-to-know-you's"
They reflect life:
Mysterious bud of youth and promise,
turning to firm and glorious prime
of color and form
before darkening ...softening... drooping...
falling utterly apart,
petal by reluctant petal.

White is purity.
I fall short.
Yellow, I think, is best—off-white,
hinting at the gracious, kind, and true.
One might aspire to yellow, for the hopes
and dreams left unfulfilled;
for the expectations of others, never met.
Still, though, a beautiful reminder
of a life fraught with humble good intentions.

LOSS (2)

"He died a hero's death, and bravely so,"
the uniformed man at the door declared.
"His country owes a debt of thanks to him,
and to you, too. We know how much you care."

He handed them the note, then slowly left.
The parents held each other tight, left numb.

The funeral was just so, with pomp and taps;
the flag presented gravely to the Mom.

The family went home, numbering three,
in mourning for the four they used to be.

TRIP

The road is never straight,
nor easy.
It rises and falls,
twists and turns,
poses challenges, ruts, and bumps.
It gets slippery and dangerous,
hot and sticky.

There are myriad intersections;
choices to make
which influence the outcome of the journey.

Often the traffic light is red,
and creates restrictions over free will.
Sometimes, it is yellow: warning, caution,
requiring decisions
about how and when to proceed.

We take on new cargo and passengers
While occasionally losing some of the old.
Adjusting and re-evaluating
are part of the daily routine.

Journey's end is sometimes abrupt:
a mishap, a flat tire, a delay.
Or, sometimes the trip continues
until we simply run out of gas.

SYMBIOSIS

The Vine said, "Tree, you stand straight,
though not as tall as once;
Bold, yet not so proud as before.
In your heyday, you were majestic, a beauty,
and generous to a fault,
providing shade and shelter, nesting nooks,
healthy air, gentle rustling peace
and calm to others.

Time has denuded you,
Stripped away your glory and dignity
as it stole your leaves, your vital fluid,
your branches.
Leaving exposed bare wood where bark once
protected your essence,
and gaping hollows where boughs had been,
now weathered away.

I am fresh supple, green.
My leaves are alive, my vine strong
and active as I cling
and climb, entwine, spread, grow.
Yet, I have needs. Might we strike a deal?

My vines grow low.
I long for sun and open space. height,
and room to spread and flourish.
You are exposed to critical eyes, even pity;
I offer to envelop you and disguise your nudity
Like a full, healthy perruque on a bald pate.
I shall lend you my color, invigorate your
appearance, revitalize your essence,
protect you from the intensity of the elements.
I will clothe you in my own growth,
full and green,
and return to you an aura of life and hope."

The Tree stood staid and mute.
The Vine did as she had promised.

SHAUNE BORNHOLDT

REVISITING THE MEADOW

The hill seems steeper than we'd thought. Familiar,
Yet strange, the old stumps rotting, and the meadow
Half overgrown now, that old shack a tangle
Of boards and grass. Two tin plates, a cracked cup.
Abandoned long ago, of course. But still
A shock. It had been standing. Did he die,

That old hunter? There is a place to die,
The nursing home in town. Someplace familiar
If not really home. Remember how he'd still
Come up here, our first years, back when
                              the meadow
Seemed young? You offered him a camping cup
Of wine, but he said he didn't want to tangle

Up his mind with liquor. Is my mind tangled
Now? Or yours? Plaque might not show, in dye,
Till later stages. No less a bitter cup.
If memory fails, can practice make familiar
The tasks of illness, if—? Now, here, this meadow
Brings waves of memories back—then, the still

Quiet air wrapped round us, absolutely still—
Cerulean sky, my hair spread in a tangle
On soft weeds, as light spread in the meadow,
Gently, and then—such joy! I thought I'd die,
But proved resilient, learning our deep familiar
Intimacies as sun poured cups and cups

Of warmth and light on us. Your hands cupped
My cheeks. Don't laugh! Well, we laughed then
                                    and still
Do, sometimes. We'd made the world familiar
With our pastimes, or so it seemed. That tangle
Of mating snakes we found! Nothing could die—
Rabbits! Chickadees! A fecund meadow.

Those stumps look mellowed in this aging meadow
Surrounded by spring flowers—buttercup,
Blue heal-all, Queen Anne's lace, the purple dye-
Spot bleeding in each center. Time distills
The drops of hope and fear. Who can untangle
The grass it glistens in, grown strange, familiar?

The hunter's shadow walks this meadow, still.
Come, love. We won't die, yet. Love's a tangle.
Let's drink the wine from our familiar cup.

THE LIFELONG LEARNING POETRY CLASS

My poem's not ready! This is really serious.
I ransack my notebooks, hoping for a find—
base metal I can alchemize in time.

Voice in my head, "Young lady, it's high time
you started homework early. There are serious
consequences in real life, you'll find."

How real was your life, Mother? Didn't you find
that cares wore down your art
                             with fractured time?
Peace, ghost. Let's make your message staunch
                                and serious.

"Stay serious. Write. You'll find it's come: *your*
                                       time."

TRAPLINE

I.

Two shapes move down-meadow—hats, dark
woolen coats.
Brother and sister are up before barn-work.

They carry a club and a burlap bag.
Small bones and beaks gleam weakly in weeds.

Stars have fallen in the wet, oozing swamp.
Slime sucks at shoes.

In flashlight beams, cattails bow their heads,
and the first trap's metal jaws flash,

clamped on a lump of blood-streaked gristle.
Here are some paw prints. Here is the pulled up
muddy stake.

Two traps on, downstream, water glistens in
thick, dark fur.
The creature stares. It makes no sound when
brother swings the club.

Its jointed paw-bones curl like babies' fingers,
ending in long claws that catch the edge of
sister's bag.

When chimney smoke swirls into gray sky, the
bag is full,
heavy, hard to haul up the long hill. Snow
begins to fall.

II.

They rinse their hands in the bucket on the porch, then wash up with soap in the kitchen sink. "Eleven is good," their mother says. Father is already in the barn, can't skin till tonight. The girl thinks the sausage on the blue plate looks like a cattail, and the pink beans look like innards. Except it's *sausage* that's innards. Eleven times fifty cents is—what? The sunny-side-up egg looks like itself and the sun and an eye all at the same time. What should its other side be called? When the pelt man comes in his rusty pickup, he'll measure each one, then throw them over the tailgate with the ones from Hensons and Clausers. Zerns comes after, she doesn't know who, then. Her brother is eating fast because he has to help with milking, but the pigs got their corn already so she can eat slow and still make the bus.

She thinks about school. They are learning the Algonquin Indians' stories, how Gitche Manitou drowned the bad people in the flood and there was nothing but water everywhere, and Nanabozho tried to dive down to get a little piece of earth to make a new world, but couldn't, even though he was a great spirit. She remembers how Loon and Mink and Turtle tried, but came up, nearly dead, and did not get the little piece of earth, and how everyone laughed at Muskrat when he said he would try. Then when he floated up dead they found a ball of mud in his paw.

III.

Black dogs leap in snow, snapping at carcasses.
High up, hung heads-down on the locust limb,
                    the brown forms stiffen.

With their outstretched forepaws, the muskrats
                    could be running or diving
but they are only dead. Small red icicles drip
                    from their mouths.

The stray dogs stop, ears pricked. They stand
                    splay-legged.
Flakes melt in breath. Snow thickens.

Now the dogs turn and trot off:
black, then gray, then white, then gone.

IV.

She thinks about how the muskrats' eyes look when she holds the flashlight, how even though she just keeps standing, there's a deep, deep place she goes each time her brother lifts the club, when she stops breathing and it feels like she is far down under something heavy. She used to get sick but not now. She dips the sausage in the sun's eye. I will be Muskrat, she thinks. Each time, I'll dive down deep and get a piece of earth to save the world. Because she must do this many times, she must not die. In her lap, her fingers curl, her nails dig into her palm. When she thinks hard she can feel the little ball of mud, wet, moving a little, like it's alive.

GLORIA WAGENKNECHT

CURLY HAIR BLUES

My curly hair has a mind of its own.
It does not obey my command.
It's brazen.
It's wild.
It never looks styled –
and rules with a firm upper hand.
I brush to the right
but it gives me a fight
and curls to the left in its stead –
And when it is done and it knows it has won
Declares itself
Head
of my head.
I'd like to have straight
and think that would be great
but, alas, I am stuck with this mane,
so I acquiesce and accept it, I guess,
and, besides,
It won't help to complain.

DAY'S END

A long, hectic day has finally come to an end. As
dusk settles in, I unlock the door and enter my
house, greeted by a tantalizing aroma of food
that has been simmering
in the slow cooker all day.
Ahhh, it's good to be home!
Dinner is ready and there is absolutely nothing
that I have to do.
All preparation was done early this morning.
I bask in a feeling of well-being, grateful
to be home and ready to enjoy my little feast.
Then I come to a realization —

Having a crock pot is like having a mother.

OUTFOXING THE SQUIRRELS

You can't outfox a squirrel
as hard as you may try.
The squirrels, just like foxes,
are shrewd and fast and sly.

These brilliant little rodents
do not accept defeat.
They twist and turn like gymnasts,
hang upside down to eat.

Consider all the money
that men and women pay
investing in bird feeders
that keep these pests away.

We purchase fancy products
alleged as "Squirrel Proof"
then find that we are victims
of outrageous retail spoof.

The baffles just don't cut it,
deterrents just don't work.
The squirrels triumph all the time
and drive us all berserk.

So, show respect for squirrels
although they make us nuts.
We just cannot outsmart them.

No ifs, no ands, no buts!

SOLAR POWER

Empowered by the source above,
I love to see its light.
My solar lamp glows brightly
and illuminates the night.

Its source is not electric
yet it shines quite brilliantly.

A marvelous invention
and it does the job for free!

ALANA SHERMAN

A PATH WINDS THROUGH SCRUB

Everything seems still
but boughs creak, leaves
scrape. The stone wall—
not breathing—
put there by living hands
is home to the always
breathing mosses quietly

green and tender to the eye.
Nothing is motionless
or noiseless in the woods.
A path winds
through scrub and ponds
whose sudden glaze of ice
reveals captured undergrowth
and frees the bitter spirit.

WHAT I FOUND

for Colette

Today at the meadow's edge
something is different.
Mossy rocks and hummocks unruly,
the well-worn path unable
to take shape this morning.
Why is a marmalade jar
half buried in the leaves?
Creamy and cracked, black letters
almost worn away, it rejects
my pocket, so I set it
in the wishbone of a tree.
Something else unforeseen—
a rusty key. Unless squirrels
have doors to their nests
it just doesn't belong
here. The key comes with me.
Where the path turns,
little ponds left over
from the last rain.
Deep or shallow, lined
with orange and brown leaves,
some have insects skidding across
their tops. I toss a pine cone
into one and watch ripples
crumple a reflected sky.

Further on a black bear cub
in the shadow of thorny brambles
stuffs plump blackberries
into its mouth.
I know its mother must be nearby
and I make a hasty detour,
then stand at the rock wall
built long ago to demarcate
woods from pasture. Tall ferns
fill the gaps. From forest glade
I cross into sunlight on the other side.

EVENSONG @ CANTERBURY

Organ music and voices
rise, saturate the great hall,
resound from stone columns.
Light streams in and song
caresses my bare shoulders.
I am a stranger here
but what I know—each person's
tale reflects something of every
other person's troubles and sins—
is clear. The vaults
make a dizzying pattern
of stars and all the intricate
glass, a mosaic of blue sky
white clouds, the green of leafy
trees leads the mind on a journey
towards center and up. I do not
care about the plaques, statues,
the stories the windows tell—they
are all a distraction
from the melody, prayer,
and the knowledge we seek;
the journey that takes us towards
ourselves in the cool stillness.

PARTICULARS

Once again essential things that astonished me as
a girl are in my thoughts: how silent
night can be, smoothness of black round
stones, heady aroma of goldenrod, rambling drift
line where ebbing tide and shore meet daily.

Light, radiant on grass, on barn roof
on puddles left by rain, on the last pink roses,
blazes from everything, even on overcast days,
with a mirrored or inherent glow
of the world we think we understand—

the sovereignty of nature: sweetness of Winesaps
weight of clouds, strength of wooden beams,
elegance of maples, feel of winter in the air—
can we come to wisdom by studying the here and
now? Our certainties shape us,
do we have any actualities?

We only need to look up to appreciate
the swirling galaxies, to ponder a perfect "V"
of geese navigating southward unerringly,
compelled by light and weather,
also feeling by reflex to come back when
magnolias blossom, all luster and blush.

IN THE KITCHEN

We wait for it to come, the time.
Jorie Graham

If you could be called back
then yes. If you could be held
in life then yes.
But brooding, befuddled I tally up your days, your
breaths—
looking for the moment where it makes sense—
what we might have said before you stopped.
There is no warning. We simply run out of time.

Everything is there and then it's not.
One Tuesday you are no longer at home.
You have no address I can give.
Where you are is too far away.

A dove is building its nest in the porch rafters.
Cooing, it flies away. Its heart beats,
it has purpose, but you are disappeared.
One small candle flickers, its light ripples.
Accept endings, accept, I say.

As you lift your hands to the sky
in a photo, I study your wrists.

A sparkling, a shimmering white
of apple blossoms
radiates forever, petals
lifted by a breeze,
scattered on grass
around the tree. "Look it's May,"
I tell you. The tall grass bends.
I see you listening.

You were born, you were in time, were outside
of time and now I am waiting
for it to go on without you. Just that.
Time will go on.
There were afternoons, moonlit highways,
the whole future. That was just yesterday.
How do I turn to the next task?

LIKE AN OCEAN WAVE

Like walking out
Into a snow-wrapped field,
You follow the fence line
or go through the woods.
You think your choice
makes a new path.
But a gray fox or some crows
have already left their tracks.
The snow glides down
your heart beats faster.

Or a wave like an ocean wave.
That curling tower tosses
a shard of blue glass—
lustrous mermaid's tears—
onto the waterline.
Every morning breakers
cough up shells
edges worn smooth.
Today you carry a stone
as old as the world
in your pocket
like a small black secret
only you know.
All opportunity and promise:
The open field
the lifting wave.

LORI MEISNER

I HAVE NOT WRITTEN

I have not written any rhymes
but those within my head.
I quite forgot what day it is,
so "Sorry, " must be said.
I cannot sit beneath a roof
while summer breathes her last.
I must be walking in the woods,
remembering weeks past,
when dandelions decked the field
and crickets sang of love.

Dandelions have gone to seed
and geese fly far above.
And so I beg forgiveness
for my absence on this day.
The rustle of the falling leaves
is calling me away
I'll be with you some time from this,
at least I'll really try
To come and sit among you
but just now my friends—goodbye!

HAIKU AND TANKA

Ezra Pound said that the poet must step away from traditional forms to avoid restriction. William Matthews maintained that when a poet becomes comfortable with his/her writing, a new approach was needed.

The Alchemy Poets undertook the writing of Haiku in an attempt to explore a new form and break away from the usual. We present the results here.

At its simplest Haiku is a seventeen syllable poem in three lines of five, seven, and five syllables. Tanka extends this to thirty-one syllables in five lines of five, seven, five, seven, and seven syllables. These definitions do not come close to expressing the complexity and depth of the forms.

Through the vivid clear writing and images of Haiku and Tanka, experience becomes alive. They teach us to build a nest for our inspiration until a reader can understand it as poetry. Haiku and Tanka give us the writer's moment and allow us as readers to share that moment.

for that brief moment
when the firefly went out
the lonely darkness
Hokushi

state your case simply
with seventeen syllables
then be done with it
gw

roadside August fields
ablaze with wild, fearless blooms
shame tamer beddings
pd

pickaxe encounters
rocks rocks rocks rocks rocks
rocks rocks
one bean-row's enough
sb

crisp days of autumn
can break the ice of winter
and cushion its blows.
gw

streaks, electric-charged
precede deep rumbling thunder
across grey-cloud sky

>mvl

far-away chainsaws
making a bee-loud buzzing
morning's alarm clock

>sb

meadow color-splashed
flowers all shapes and sizes
flourish together

>mvl

swirling dervishes
carried by strong winter gusts
dance on lakes and fields
frenzied snow-ghosts leap aloft
dissipate into thin air

                              mvl

sharp scent of forest
cabs whiz buses go crawling
past trussed tilted pines

                              sb

strawberry's blossoms
disguise themselves as clover
birds wait for the fruit

                              as

fuzzy catkins rest
along lithe stem of willow
wait for leaves to pop
                    mvl

the grass is greener
for the saying of green.
green beneath starlings crows
                as

comes a puff of air
fallen leaves begin to dance
swirl and pirouette
buoyant in the easy wind
autumn leaves perform ballet
                gw

anger guilt sadness
acceptance move on alone
years pass void remains
                    mms

heron shoulders hunched
stands like bearded Confucius
long hair-like feathers
flowing 'cross his chest and back
watching motionless for fish
                    mvl

winter nights hard with
bitter wind splinters of glass
glittering in tar
like the moon's image resting
on cold silent country ponds
                    as

swirling on sidewalks
millions of green ginkgo leaves
autumn's gold stolen
                    sb

                    spiders weave silky webs
                    that span the dark forest sky
                    catching luna light
                            pd

autumn treetops blaze
a gold and russet morning
earth's seasonal praise
                            as

ABOUT THE AUTHORS

Vera Atkins is from Neversink, New York. Vera has been writing her delightful poems based on family, values and nature for many years.

Shaune Bornholdt grew up in rural Pennsylvania, lives in New York City, and spends much of her time in the Catskills. Her poems have been published in *American Arts Quarterly, The Wallace Stevens Journal, Mezzo Cammin* and other journals.

Patricia Durney A long-time resident of Sullivan County, Patricia is a retired teacher. In addition to writing poetry, Patricia enjoys painting.

P.R Gates born in DeWitt, NY, currently lives in the house that her grandfather built in 1939. Since retiring from New Hope Community, she spends her time quilting, gardening, writing, and volunteering. at both the Time and the Valleys Museum and the Daniel Pierce library. She is a member of The 1st Friday Book Club.

Marilyn Vasko Laufer is a lifelong resident of Sullivan County. Now retired, Marilyn has more time to devote to writing poetry, as well as nature photography. She is Poet Laureate of Liberty, New York.

Lori Meisner (1945-2019) was a resident of Sullivan County for more than 40 years. An archeologist and horse trainer, in February she was killed when she was kicked by an unruly mare. She will be missed.

Marcia M. Salton is a full time resident of White Lake, NY, is a retired corporate executive. She lives on White Lake, which is a constant inspiration for poetry and prose. Writing has always been a very special and satisfying means of expression.

Cora Schwartz a retired psychologist, combined her professional experiences with the true story of her 25-year love affair to create *GYPSY TEARS, LOVING A HOLOCAUST SURVIVOR*. She is also the author and photographer of *THE FORGOTTEN FEW*. Cora is presently working on a sequel to *GYPSY TEARS*

Alana Sherman poet, teacher and editor, resides and works in Woodbourne, New York. Widely published, Alana is the author of three books of poetry and two childrens' books, most recently *THE BUNNIES OF FOX RUN FARM*.

Gloria Wagenknecht lives in Loch Sheldrake, New York. Her photographs and poetry are about wildlife and the rural beauty of Sullivan County. Gloria's work has appeared in Audubon publications and earlier Alchemy Books.